THE
STRATEGY
POCKETBOOK

By Neil Russell-Jones
Drawings by Phil Hailstone

2009001656

Published by:
Management Pocketbooks Ltd
Laurel House, Station Approach, Alresford, Hants SO24 9JH, U.K.
Tel: +44 (0)1962 735573   Fax: +44 (0)1962 733637
E-mail: sales@pocketbook.co.uk
Website: www.pocketbook.co.uk

This edition published 2005. Reprinted 2007, 2009.

© Neil Russell-Jones 2005.

British Library Cataloguing-in-Publication Data – A catalogue record for this book is available from the British Library.

ISBN 978 1 903776 13 1

Design, typesetting and graphics by **efex ltd**. Printed in U.K.

CONTENTS

1NTRODUCTION

STRATEGY: DEVELOPING KEY SKILLS

> '...Strategy... has often come to be synonymous with the quantitative breakthrough, the analytic coup, market share numbers, learning curve, theory, positioning business in a 4- or 9- or 24-box matrix... and putting it all on a computer.'
>
> **Peters and Waterman**,
> *In Search of Excellence.*

This book is about strategy. It will not make you a strategy expert, nor will it enable you to be a strategic 'guru'. It will, however, explain the basics of strategy so that you should be able to understand the key components of a strategy, how to approach setting and developing a strategy, and some of the strategic tools that can be used.

It will also help you:

- Understand what strategy 'experts' might be saying
- Assist you in challenging what others say

STRATEGY: DEVELOPING KEY SKILLS

This book should be read by: people in business who need to develop a more formalised strategy than perhaps hitherto; staff partially or indirectly involved in strategy; and students and others who wish an overview to serve as a framework on which they can build. Stakeholders in an organisation will also find it useful.

A lot is written about strategy – some of it arcane and some very complex. This book will cut through that. The book considers some basic strategic terms, explains the difference between competitive and corporate strategy (a major cause of confusion at some surprisingly senior executive levels) and sets out a simple approach to strategic development.

INTRODUCTION

SOME STRATEGIC TERMS

Vision	The long-range idea that drives the organisation
Mission	The essence of the strategy
Stakeholders	Those entities and people who have an interest in the success of a strategy
Critical Success Factors (CSFs)	Those things that are essential for success
Corporate strategy	The long-term goals for the organisation as a whole
Competitive strategy	The long-term goals for specific markets and offerings
Segment	A sub-set of a market
Customer Value Proposition (CVP)	The offering for each specified market, or segment
Competitive edge	What sets you apart from the competition

INTRODUCTION

WHAT IS STRATEGY?

A dictionary definition is: 'Generalship or the art of conducting a campaign or manoeuvring an army; artifice or finesse generally.' – from Greek *stratēgos* (general) from *stratos* (army) and *agein* (to lead). ***Chambers***.

Leading 'business gurus' define it as:

'The essence of strategic thinking is about creating a sustainable competitive advantage.'
Porter, *article in The Economist, 1987.*

'(Business) strategy... concerns major decisions deliberately taken to establish what sets of customers a business aims to serve in the future and against what competition, in order to meet its financial objectives.'
Mathur and Kenyon, *Creating Value.*

'Strategy...is not enough to optimally position a company within existing markets; the challenge is to... develop great foresight into the whereabouts of tomorrow's markets.'
Hamel and Prahalad, *Competing for the Future, 1996.*

WHAT IS STRATEGY?

DEFINITION

However, it is quite simply:

… the development of a set of unique and irreproducible competencies and customer value propositions that enable you to continue to generate value…

'Competencies' in this case means those things that your organisation does in order to carry out its business. It is a mixture of people, systems, structure and skills, culture, distribution and operations etc.

If the competencies are reproducible then they will be copied by your competitors and you will lose your competitive edge.

A strategy, therefore, is a statement that defines which markets you will be in and sets out the organisational competencies that you will need (and what actions you need to take to develop them) to enable you to gain and sustain your competitive edge – ie to persuade customers to buy from you rather than the competition.

WHAT IS STRATEGY?

FOCUS

Organisations exist for different reasons and the reasons that cause them to come into existence will drive their culture – how they work (sometimes called 'ethos') etc. Organisations that have as their vision worthy ideals such as…

- To end world poverty
- To eradicate leprosy
- To succour world hunger

… will have vastly different approaches, stakeholders and measures than commercial organisations whose objectives are, inter alia, to generate returns on capital.

A mutual organisation (eg building society, co-operative) will also differ from a commercial bank or major quoted retailer in that its principal duties (theoretically) lie to its members who are also its owners. Notwithstanding this, each will (should) have a vision and therefore must have a strategy since that strategy is the means to achieve the vision. It is the emphasis placed on different aspects and the relationships with stakeholders that cause the differences.

WHAT DOES A CORPORATE STRATEGY DO?

Strategy takes the **vision** and develops it into a framework and translates it into a
set of actions, ie steps for achieving the vision (or at least attempting that) – see following
diagram. For a commercial organisation this will revolve around *creating* and then
sustaining/increasing value (equity). To this end strategy:

- Sets long-term objectives
- Drives actions
- Gives resource allocation priorities
- Defines the competency domain of the organisation
- Leads to core competency development through
  - competitive strategies
  - functional policies
- Is simple to grasp
- Is flexible enough to respond to *force majeure* but changes must be defined,
  discussed and definitely agreed – not drifted into
- Is viable

WHAT A STRATEGY DOES

Translates gap analysis between **vision** and **today** into a series of actions to get there. You must understand the key market issues and what you are good at:

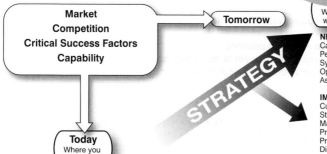

Market
Competition
Critical Success Factors
Capability

Tomorrow

VISION
Where you want to be

STRATEGY

Today
Where you are now

NEEDS
Capital
People
Systems
Operating Procedures
Assets

IMPLIES
Culture
Structure
Marketing
Products
Pricing
Distribution

CORPORATE TIME HORIZONS

The diagram opposite shows the different time horizons that relate to each component of strategy. The very top, and the most abstract, is the **vision**, which is very long term and is supported by the **corporate rules** that govern how an organisation operates in a general sense, eg:

- The return rate on capital that is required (ROCE)
- The Key Performance Indicators (KPIs, or measures)
- Ethical considerations, etc

These things do not really change much or radically over time – but will respond to longer-term requirements.

The **mission** is more tangible and shorter in time (3–5 years), supported by details of the **strategy** and **functional policies**. These are in turn supported by **plans** (activities to be carried out now) and **budgets** (looking at money needed to carry out those activities and the revenues that they will generate) which tend to be short term (1–3 years) and very concrete.

CORPORATE TIME HORIZONS

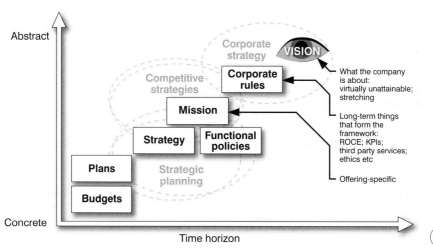

Abstract

Corporate strategy

VISION

Corporate rules

What the company is about: virtually unattainable; stretching

Competitive strategies

Mission

Long-term things that form the framework: ROCE; KPIs; third party services; ethics etc

Strategy

Functional policies

Offering-specific

Plans

Strategic planning

Budgets

Concrete

Time horizon

STRATEGY: A SUMMARY

In general:

- Strategy is deliberate – not accidental
- It is forward looking – you cannot manage the past
- It is about stakeholder satisfaction
- It is all embracing
- A strategy deals with the 'organisation as a whole' not the 'whole organisation'
- It is the articulation of the **vision**, in so far as it is possible, in a way that can be understood
- It sets goals that can be measured

There can only be one **corporate strategy**, but there can be, and often are, several **competitive strategies**, depending on the constituent parts of the organisation.

STRATEGIC COMPONENTS

KEY ELEMENTS

This chapter will explore the key components of strategy.

 It will consider the difference between corporate and competitive strategy, where much of the confusion that surrounds strategy arises, and the major parts of each.

 It will look at the factors that will affect and drive how strategy is shaped and who has inputs into strategy.

 The major groups of stakeholders are considered and why it is necessary to understand them and have measures for each group in relation to the fundamental strategic objectives…

FUNDAMENTAL STRATEGIC OBJECTIVES

For a commercial organisation the **fundamental objective** is to earn a return on capital that is *greater than the cost of that capital*. Thus it can continue to have the right to use that capital and, if necessary, have the right to raise more to meet its vision. All other objectives are **means objectives** in support of that fundamental objective.

Corporate strategy* is, therefore, about managing the **value** of an organisation – often expressed in monetary or financial terms. Thus it is helpful to refer to this as **financial value**.

Competitive strategy* is about assembling the *inputs* (raw materials, assets, people, technology, finance, distribution) which, when put together with reference to a defined market as a **Customer Value Proposition (CVP)**, enable the *outputs* (products/services) to be delivered to the market for **commercial value**.

Support strategies are in fact components of the competitive strategy (or strategies) and it is more helpful to refer to them as **functional policies** as they usually refer to a particular organisational function such as HR, IT, Finance etc.

* NB: note the difference between these two!

(19)

CORPORATE VS COMPETITIVE STRATEGY

There are key differences between the two types of strategies, as shown below:

	Corporate Strategy	Competitive Strategy
Overarching Statement	Vision	Mission
Level	• Top – broadest view • Looks out, up, down and across • Sets general goals	• Management level • Focuses on markets • Sets specific goals
Resources	• Sets priorities	• Allocates
Focus	• Financial	• Commercial
Products	• Relates to them in a general sense • May own corporate brand	• At the heart of the strategy • Owns specific product brands

Most thinking and analysis focuses on **competitive** strategy as this delivers to the **corporate** strategy. Functional policies support these.

VISION VS MISSION

These terms are often used indiscriminately and confusingly, along with other terms such as *goals*, *objectives* and *targets*. As a result they do not act as guides and frameworks for organisations and often end up as trite, useless and generic statements.

To clarify things it is better to adopt separate and discrete meanings:

Vision *(very few organisations really have this)*

- An initially almost unmeasurable idea that should provide unity of purpose and inspire

- It should be uncluttered, eg 'Put a man on Mars' (NASA); 'A PC on every desk' (Microsoft); 'Quality, service, cleanliness and value' (McDonald's); 'A GI to buy soda anywhere in the world' (Coke)

- It does not talk about markets or targets and it is durable, ie it does not change unless there is catastrophic change in the world

STRATEGIC COMPONENTS

VISION VS MISSION

Mission

Relates to an entity or a service offering; sits within the vision – ie is a step along the way. Is market-focused and contains high-level goals and targets…

Goals (= objectives)

The aims you must get right to satisfy your stakeholders/customers and to meet your corporate requirements. By achieving your goals you know when you have arrived (strategically speaking). They must be differentiated from…

Targets

Through which you **measure your achievement** relative to goals and which drive corporate behaviour. Targets can be cascaded down an organisation to ensure unity of effort.

STRATEGIC CONSIDERATIONS

A **corporate strategy** will consider:

- Business segmentation
- Branding at the corporate level
- Capital strategy
- Vertical integration (eg buying suppliers/distributors)
- Group HR policies
- Corporate positioning
- Corporate philosophy
- Delegated autonomy
- 'Portfolio management' (internal)
- Horizontal co-operation (across the organisation)

Competitive strategy, however, looks at different issues...

CORPORATE
vs
COMPETITIVE

STRATEGIC QUESTIONS

There are some basic questions that
a **competitive strategy** must answer:

- What does the market want?
- What are we going to offer?
- How are we going to offer it?
- At what do we need to excel to succeed?
- How will the competition respond?
- Can we make money?
- What are the internal implications?
- What do we need to change?
- Will we satisfy our stakeholders?
- What are the risks and how shall we manage them?

FACTORS SHAPING COMPETITIVE STRATEGY

There are three groups of factors that affect a competitive strategy:

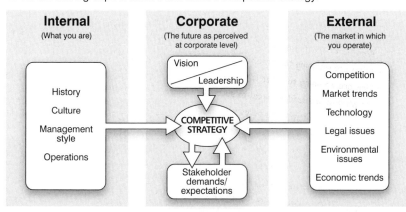

Internal
(What you are)

History

Culture

Management style

Operations

Corporate
(The future as perceived at corporate level)

Vision / Leadership

COMPETITIVE STRATEGY

Stakeholder demands/expectations

External
(The market in which you operate)

Competition

Market trends

Technology

Legal issues

Environmental issues

Economic trends

FACTORS SHAPING COMPETITIVE STRATEGY

INTERNAL

The following factors shape the organisation and how it functions:

- What you have done before – the products and market in which you operate
- Your existing customers – and those that you have lost!
- The history of the organisation and the path that led up to where it is
- Culture – how things are done – the unwritten and implicit ways of working or behaving
- Market perception – what customers and competitors think of you and your offerings
- Inherited assets – legacy systems; people; processes; supplier relationships; stakeholders; management style; structure and infrastructure

Any attempt to carry out strategy that is contrary to several of these factors is doomed to failure unless the organisation changes to meet this.

STRATEGIC COMPONENTS

FACTORS SHAPING COMPETITIVE STRATEGY

CORPORATE

The future as perceived by the executive:

- The **vision** that pertains – what drives the organisation

- The style and effectiveness of **leadership** – dictatorial; cohesive and open; or new and therefore 'sweeping clean'

- The **stakeholder demands** that drive the organisation – the different and sometimes conflicting demands that are made by *inter alia*: staff; management; shareholders; the board; local communities; governments; pressure groups; unions; members if a co-op or mutual

- The **philosophy** of the organisation – whether it is a conglomerate (Hanson; BET); whether it is fairly acquisitive (GE, KKR) whether it sticks with one thing (Southwest Airlines, McDonald's); and whether it integrates horizontally, vertically forward or vertically backwards, or both

- The relative **brand strength** – eg Nestlé has a portfolio of very strong product brands such as Maggi or Kit-Kat under the Nestlé umbrella, whereas generally Ford vehicles are Fords with a name: Ford Ka or Ford Capri (but not Jaguar which is branded separately)

FACTORS SHAPING COMPETITIVE STRATEGY

EXTERNAL

No organisation is an island and strategy must take cognisance of the trends and the outside players and how they will react:

- **Changing market demands** – which must be recognised and a response developed
- **Competitive actions and responses** – what competitors are doing and also how they will react to what you might do. If you cut your prices, a large competitor might respond by slashing theirs and, with deeper pockets than yours, force you out of business

STRATEGIC COMPONENTS

FACTORS SHAPING COMPETITIVE STRATEGY

EXTERNAL

- **Legal issues** – which will affect what you can and cannot do: eg compliance in financial services, Health and Safety

- **Environmental trends** – which will force changes in what you can do, even if there is no legal requirement (eg BP's change of logo and colour to green to reflect a greater perceived environmental awareness)

- **Economic and demographic trends** – eg changes in disposable income, altering age profiles, increasing tendency for single-parent families, increase in private pensions in some markets

- **Technological trends** – internet, faster pace of development and therefore technological obsolescence, centralising of processing to regional/global hubs with consequent decrease in costs and increase in service

ACHIEVING STRATEGY

It is not always possible to achieve strategy, or you may only be partially successful, because many factors operate against this:

- The markets may change (demand, regulation)
- The implementation may take too long
- Competitors change their game plan
- New technology makes old operations obsolescent

These factors push the strategy off course – known as strategic drift (see later).

In addition there are several different ways (some more successful than others) in which **strategy** becomes **fact**, as the following diagram shows.

PATTERNS OF STRATEGIC DEVELOPMENT

There are various ways that strategy develops depending on several factors:

Straight line continuum

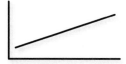

Unco-ordinated

Step changes

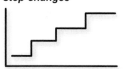

Fundamental transformation

STRATEGIC DRIFT

When reviewing a strategy commentators frequently imply that it was a deliberate act of management. This is, in reality, very rarely 100% the case. Typically there is a difference in the 'desired' strategy and that which is actually 'realised'.

This is, of course, due to the fact that a strategy is largely a **theoretical** long-term plan for getting to some point based on assumptions (supported by robust analysis and clear conclusions).

In the real world, however, competitors, customers and other entities (eg governments) tend not to conform to your predictions about behaviours. As a result actions in response to this and the resulting impacts cause the realised strategy to differ from the desired one.

In addition, failure to implement fully or properly will tend to cause differences to emerge – ie the strategy '**drifts**'. The following diagram shows this.

STRATEGIC DRIFT

Strategic drift occurs where factors combine to stop an organisation from attaining its intended strategic position.

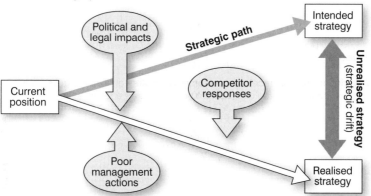

NOTES

STAKEHOLDERS

WHY CONSIDER STAKEHOLDERS?

In essence a strategy is an articulation of the path to a vision – one that is consciously accepted by stakeholders (or else they will not support it). Stakeholders can have one or more of the following roles...

Legislator	• Government/EU • Regulatory body	**Consumer**	• Customers • Distributors
Influencer	• Community • Government • Pressure group • Union	**Enabler**	• Staff • Equity providers • Distributors • Suppliers • Third party suppliers

... and they often have different (sometimes conflicting) demands.

CORPORATE STRATEGY

STAKEHOLDER INPUTS

	Involvement	Ability to Influence	Detail
CEO	High	Highest	Full
Top Team	High	High	Full
Management	Low	Low	Most
Employees	Low	Lowest	Part
Stakeholders	Low/Medium	Medium/High	Low

Different players will have greater or lesser inputs depending on their ability to influence.
Key issues – how, what and when to communicate.

STAKEHOLDERS

WHO ARE THE STAKEHOLDERS?

Primary:

- Customers
- Employees
- Investors

Others:

- Bondholders and lenders
- Market analysts
- Regulators and government bodies
- Competitors
- Suppliers
- Pressure groups

What keeps stakeholders committed to working with an organisation?...

STAKEHOLDER VALUE DRIVES BEHAVIOUR

Stakeholders stay committed to the relationship when they receive more Stakeholder Value Output (SVo) – however they define it – than the Stakeholder Value Input that they deliver (SVi): ie SVo > SVi. For some this output will be financial, for others a combination of things (service, benefits, convenience etc). Your strategy must take this into account.

VALUE ADDED MODEL

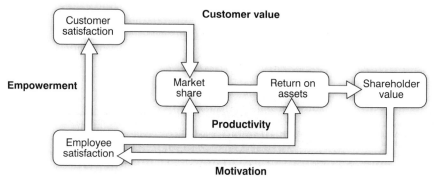

This model, as developed and used by Rank Xerox, demonstrates the linkages between key sets of stakeholders – employees, customers and shareholders – in generating value. It exemplifies that it is important to consider all stakeholders (although not necessarily in the same proportion) when formulating strategies.

MAJOR STAKEHOLDER GROUPS

An organisation must generate value that meets the requirements of all major stakeholders.

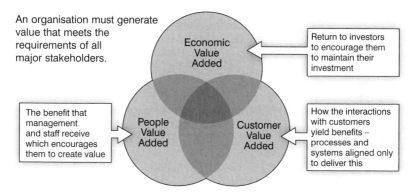

Economic Value Added

Return to investors to encourage them to maintain their investment

People Value Added

The benefit that management and staff receive which encourages them to create value

Customer Value Added

How the interactions with customers yield benefits – processes and systems aligned only to deliver this

To demonstrate how you are meeting stakeholder requirements it is necessary to develop a suite of measures that do this.

MEASUREMENT

If the corporate strategy sets the overall goals and the competitive strategy sets them in relation to offerings, it is important to know whether or not you are achieving them and thus delivering value. To this end, therefore, some degree of **measurement** is needed.

It is necessary to quantify all goals by setting the targets that must be measured. These quantified targets are known as the **Key Performance Indicators** (KPIs) and must be set for all aspects of the organisation to enable you to measure success (or failure!). They must measure all aspects of operations and should focus on:

- **Measures for customer excellence** that demonstrate how you are delivering your goods in terms of value
- **Measures for stakeholders**, with the principal classes being management and staff and suppliers of capital
- **Internal measures for excellence** which tell executives how well the organisation is performing

STRATEGIC PHASES

The key phases that must be undertaken – whichever 'philosophy' you or your organisation follow – are:

- Develop the vision
- Understand what that means for stakeholders
- Set the corporate strategy
- Formulate competitive strategies
- Develop the functional policies
- Prepare five-year plan
- Crystallise current plan

The next chapter will explore these.

NOTES

STRATEGIC STEPS

CONCEPTS OF ANALYSIS

Although there are many proprietary approaches to strategic analysis they can be reduced down to the same simple concepts. It is the emphasis or method of supporting analysis that differs. The basic steps are:

- Primary analysis (of you, your competition, the market)
- Secondary analysis (of your offering and what it means for you to offer it)
- Planning
- Implementing

This can be broken down as per the diagram opposite.

(Strategic 'tools' referred to are explained in the next chapter. The templates used here are examples. There are many variations – you may wish to derive your own.)

DEVELOPMENT PROCESS

COMPETITIVE STRATEGY

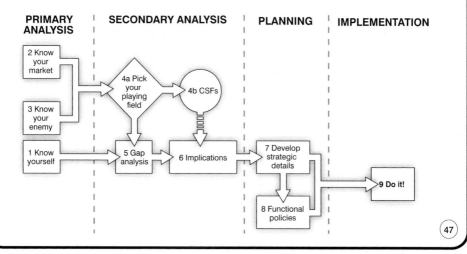

| PRIMARY ANALYSIS | SECONDARY ANALYSIS | PLANNING | IMPLEMENTATION |

- 2 Know your market
- 3 Know your enemy
- 1 Know yourself
- 4a Pick your playing field
- 4b CSFs
- 5 Gap analysis
- 6 Implications
- 7 Develop strategic details
- 8 Functional policies
- 9 Do it!

1 KNOW YOURSELF

Key points – You cannot manage those things that are outside of your control (customers, competition) but you might, however, be able to **influence** those external factors. Understanding this will be a powerful force in shaping your strategy. Conversely, internal factors can (should) be more easily managed, but they also constrain what you can do. For example, you cannot mine gold unless you have access to a mine and you cannot programme software if you have no developers. Implicit in this are the changes that must be made to facilitate delivery of the strategy.

Key questions – What are we good at? Where are we weak? Why is that the case? What are our key goals? What is our vision?

Actions – Analyse your company, critically and objectively. This involves qualitative (SWOT see page 82) and quantitative (numbers) analysis. Agree/revisit goals and formulate/review vision.

Tools – SWOT, Business Impact Analysis and Scenario Analysis to see how things might change and whether your SWOT items remain the same (hold strategic workshops).

1 KNOW YOURSELF

VISION AND GOALS

The first thing that must be achieved – if your organisation doesn't have it already – is the vision and the supporting goals.

The vision, as discussed, is the statement that is the essence of what you are about and which should inspire your staff, customers and stakeholders. The goals are the things that you need to achieve to hit the vision and are imperatives for the business. They fall into three areas:

- **Customer goals** – what are the things that we must do to ensure that we are our customers' preferred choice?
- **Stakeholder goals** – what must we do to delight our stakeholders (management, staff, shareholders/members, board, regulators, communities etc)?
- **Excellence goals** – what must we excel at to gain and maintain competitive advantage?

Goals should be exciting, challenging and described in the present tense...

STRATEGIC STEPS

1 KNOW YOURSELF
GOALS FOR CUSTOMERS

Customer goals express, in simple language, why customers **prefer to do business with you**.

- Have 1–4 goals
- Include a superlative or qualifier

Examples:

- Customers believe that our products are the best value for money
- Our customers receive an efficient and friendly service
- Our products are flexible and meet our customers' needs

STRATEGIC STEPS

1 KNOW YOURSELF

GOALS FOR STAKEHOLDERS

What you must do to **delight your stakeholders**.

Stakeholders include shareholders/members, staff, management, board, regulators and, possibly, local communities (difficult to measure).

- Have 2–6 goals
- Include something about being a great company to work for
- Include staff development
- Include solvency/liquidity if appropriate
- Include financial goals – eg return on mean assets

Examples:

- Market share is 20% or better in our chosen markets
- Our expense ratio is in the top three of our peer group
- Our staff turnover is half that of the industry
- Return on capital in top ten percentile for industry

STRATEGIC STEPS

1 KNOW YOURSELF

GOALS FOR EXCELLENCE

These goals should focus on the core competencies of the organisation. **At what must you excel?**

- Have between 6–8 goals which should include:
  - product development
  - distribution/delivery
  - information
  - operations

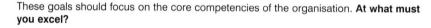

Examples:

- We understand our markets better than our competitors
- Managers receive the right management information to enable them to manage the resources at their disposal

1 KNOW YOURSELF

TARGETS

Have 1–3 targets per goal.

- Consider how you will measure attainment of your goals
- Quantify targets in some way
- If necessary, develop new measures
- Ensure targets form an essential input to board meetings going forward

Examples:

- Market share is 20% or better in our chosen markets, eg:
  - compound growth of 12% pa
  - improved profitability to 17% pre-tax
- Customers believe that our products are the best value for money, eg:
  - consistently in the top five in independent surveys
  - increased retention rates to 85%

- We understand our markets better than our competitors, eg:
  - we carry out two annual surveys into potential clients
  - we focus on our target customers who make up 80% of our client base defined by monetary value
- Our expense ratio is in the top three of our peers, eg:
  - expenses ratio is 0.9% or better

1 KNOW YOURSELF

GOALS AND TARGETS

You can use this template to draw up the **goals** and **targets** to quantify or measure progress with your customer (or stakeholder or excellence) goals. Then you can start your analysis.

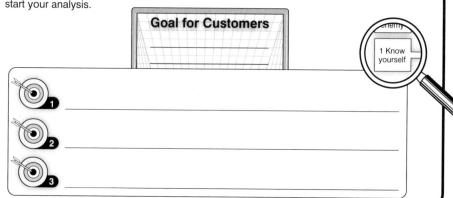

STRATEGIC STEPS

2 KNOW YOUR MARKET

Key points – This is about understanding the market dynamics, ie the shape and progress of your market, the trends now and in the future. For example:

How is technology affecting it? What are customers demanding? What regulations are emerging? What products or services are coming onto the map? How is distribution changing (clicks vs bricks)? How is the competition structured? You must look forward as you will be competing in the future.

Key questions – Who buys what, where and how (branch vs internet vs sales force, etc)? What are government views? Who are our customers? How have they changed?

Actions – Understand why customers buy from you (and why some don't). Analyse why disaffected customers left. Analyse the trends and changes.

Tools – PESTLE (see page 83), market research, analysis of customer base, exit interviews, scenario analysis, segmentation.

2 KNOW YOUR MARKET

FACTORS FOR ANALYSIS

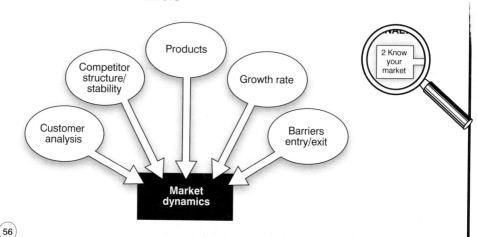

2 KNOW YOUR MARKET

THE IMPACT OF BARRIERS ON PROFIT

Barriers have an impact on a firm's operations. **Entry barriers** (copyrights, patents, investment requirements, knowledge, legislation) keep competition out and can lead to higher profits. **Exit barriers** (disinvestment, legislation, redundancy costs etc) can stop players exiting when they should and, therefore, cause instability. Understanding these is a key component of strategic formulation.

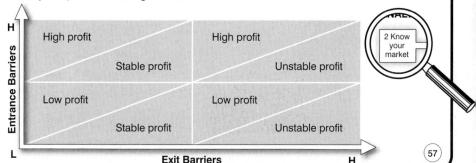

2 KNOW YOUR MARKET

SEGMENTATION

Although you may have a competitive advantage, it is not possible to achieve this in every aspect of the market. Consequently, it is important to split the market into segments and decide on those where you will do best.

A segment can be defined as one in which:

Or, it can be described as:

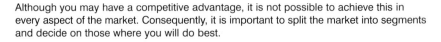

'Members will respond in a similar manner (more or less) to marketing stimuli'

'Distinct groups of buyers with similar needs, characteristics or behaviour who might require separate products or marketing mixes'

2 Know your market

You must therefore...

2 KNOW YOUR MARKET

SEGMENTATION

Decide on what bases you will segment, ie:

- Analyse the attractiveness of those segments for you
- Decide in which segments you will make money and prioritise them
- Choose the position of your offerings in those segments
- Develop your Customer Value Propositions (CVPs) for each

Segments chosen should be those where **you can make money**. This implies that you must:

- Understand the market better
- Have a better offering than your competitors
- Tailor it more specifically to wants and needs or
- Be able to deliver it at a lower cost

Example segments are shown on the next page.

2 KNOW YOUR MARKET

SEGMENTATION – GENERAL STRATEGIES

Based on the segment attractiveness (whether you can make money) and the strength of your CVP (how much better your offering is than the competition) there are a number of generic competitive strategic initiatives that can be followed.

3 KNOW YOUR ENEMY

Key points – This is about finding out who your major competitors are now – and who they will be in the future (they may not be the same as in the past, they may not even be from the same industry) – and establishing your **competitive position** (see later).

Key questions – Who does our customer base go to? If not to us, why not? To whom might they go in the future? What product/service differences are there, now and in the future? Who might enter, who might withdraw and why? What are the barriers to entry or exit?

Actions – Analyse the competition now/future. Understand why you succeeded (or failed!). Establish what will be important in the future. Carry out product comparisons.

Tools – Porter's five forces, competitive research (databases, internet etc), competitive feature/benefit comparison.

3 KNOW YOUR ENEMY

SUN TZU MATRIX

By understanding yourself vis-à-vis the competition you have a greater chance of success.

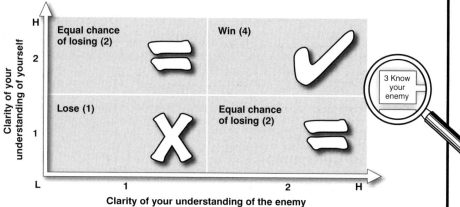

3 KNOW YOUR ENEMY
ESTABLISH COMPETITIVE POSITION

Having understood past position (A) and analysed the requirements for future success (B) it will be possible to establish your future competitive position (C) in your chosen segments.

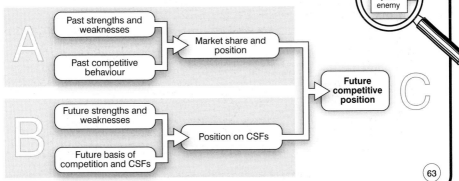

3 KNOW YOUR ENEMY

UNDERSTAND YOUR COMPETITORS

By comparing major players' market share and looking at the trends, you can get a view as to how the market is moving.

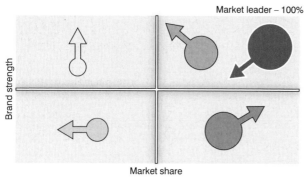

Market leader – 100%

Brand strength

Market share

Player with share expressed as % market leader and direction player is moving

3 Know your enemy

4a PICK YOUR PLAYING FIELD

Key points – This is about understanding exactly where you have the competitive edge and then focusing on those areas (known as segments) where you can exploit your advantages.

Key questions – Who buys what, where and how (branch vs internet vs sales force etc)? Where do we have the advantage? How do we keep it? In which segments can we maximise money?

Actions – Decide on which segments you will focus. Develop a unique Customer Value Proposition (that sets out a clear message to the customers of the benefits to them from choosing you).

Tools – Segment analysis, market research, trend analysis.

4a Pick your playing field

4b CSFs

COMPETING

In understanding the market you must know how players compete and what Critical Success Factors (CSFs) you must be good at in order to compete (win).

Basis of competition	Ranking	Implied Critical Success Factor
Price	1	Low-cost operations
Distribution	5	Multi channels
Service	4	Superb training
etc	2	etc
etc	3	etc

4b CSFs

5 GAP ANALYSIS

Key points – This is about understanding what you need to be successful in your chosen segments and where you need to improve your capabilities (see following diagram).

Key questions – Where are we weak? Where is our competition strong… or changing? What does this imply?

Actions – Contrast your success and failures with those of the current and future competition. Determine the CSFs in those chosen markets (see previous page).

Tools – Porter's five forces, competitive research (databases, internet etc), competitive feature/benefit comparison, CSF analysis.

5 GAP ANALYSIS

Compare yourself with your competition (best in class) and then identify the gaps in performance.

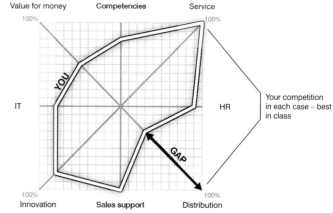

Value for money
Competencies
Service
100%
100%

YOU

IT

HR

Your competition in each case – best in class

100%
100%

Innovation
Sales support
Distribution

GAP

5 Gap analysis

5 GAP ANALYSIS

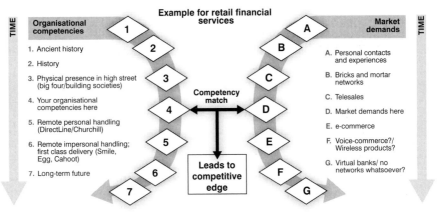

Example for retail financial services

TIME

Organisational competencies

1. Ancient history
2. History
3. Physical presence in high street (big four/building societies)
4. Your organisational competencies here
5. Remote personal handling (DirectLine/Churchill)
6. Remote impersonal handling; first class delivery (Smile, Egg, Cahoot)
7. Long-term future

Market demands

TIME

A. Personal contacts and experiences
B. Bricks and mortar networks
C. Telesales
D. Market demands here
E. e-commerce
F. Voice-commerce?/ Wireless products?
G. Virtual banks/ no networks whatsoever?

Competency match

Leads to competitive edge

As long as your organisation has the competency demanded by the market then you can achieve competitive edge. If they go out of sync, however...

69

5 GAP ANALYSIS: MIS-MATCH

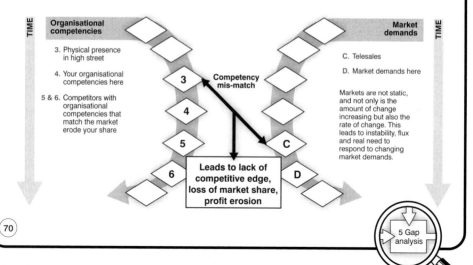

Organisational competencies

3. Physical presence in high street

4. Your organisational competencies here

5 & 6. Competitors with organisational competencies that match the market erode your share

Market demands

C. Telesales

D. Market demands here

Markets are not static, and not only is the amount of change increasing but also the rate of change. This leads to instability, flux and real need to respond to changing market demands.

Competency mis-match

Leads to lack of competitive edge, loss of market share, profit erosion

TIME

70

5 Gap analysis

6 IMPLICATIONS

Key points – From the analysis, what are the key issues that impact on your organisation? What do you need to do to improve them? (See following diagram.)

Key questions – What do we need to change? How do we change it? By when should we change, and how much? Can we do it alone, or do we need help?

Actions – Develop plans to attack the key issues and think through the implications. Cost vs revenue… is it worth it? What disruption might be caused? When would it pay back? Is it sustainable?

Tools – Planning, scenario planning, change management, business case development/quantification, budgeting.

6 Implications

6 IMPLICATIONS

CSFs

Your current position

Can we deliver?
Can we make money?

Implications for the organisation:

- Can we do this?
- What must we change?
- What should we buy-in/outsource?
- What skills do we need?
- Can our systems/processes cope?
- Is our structure right?
- Do we have the right distribution channels?
- Are our costs in sync?

6 Implications

7 DEVELOP THE STRATEGIC DETAILS

Key points – These are the tactics and actions that you must put in hand to achieve your objectives. Too often these are overlooked and therefore organisations fail to achieve the strategic goals.

Key questions – Which parts of our organisation do we need to change? What budgets do we need? What plans?

Actions – Cascade strategic goals down to all parts of the organisation:

- Allocate responsibilities, milestones, deadlines
- Quantify outcomes – impact on B/S, P&L, cashflow

7 Develop strategic details

Tools – Budgets, planning, RACI analysis, core competency analysis.

7 DEVELOP THE STRATEGIC DETAILS

DEFINING THE DETAILS

The offering	• What do customers need?
	• Are customers interested?
	• Do they see value in the proposition?
Size the prize	• Who are the target customers?
	• What revenues are there?
	• How sustainable are they?
Getting ready	• What is the long-term game?
	• What assets and strengths do we have already to exploit this opportunity?
	• What additional technical/content capabilities are needed?
Winning	• Who are, or will be, our competitors?
	• How will we beat them?
	• What are the risks and how do we manage them?
Distribution	• How do we get into this market/improve current position?
	• Who might we ally with?
	• Who might we acquire?

7 Develop strategic details

8 FUNCTIONAL POLICIES

Key points – This is about developing the policies for the support functions (HR, IT, Marketing, Finance etc) that will underpin the strategy.

Key questions – Where must we strengthen our support areas? What skills/systems do we need? Is our structure correct to carry out the strategy?

Actions – Review training, analyse financing, review IT strategy, set marketing goals as sub-set of competitive strategies.

Tools – Iterative challenges, budgetary analysis and development, planning.

8 FUNCTIONAL POLICIES

COMPETITIVE STRATEGY AND SUPPORTING, FUNCTIONAL POLICIES

The competitive strategy, whilst unique to each offering, is of course a blend of the offering and the supporting functional policies.

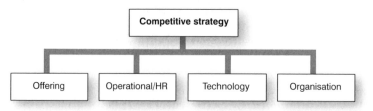

8 Functional policies

8 FUNCTIONAL POLICIES

STRUCTURE

Structure is an extremely important issue. The wrong structure can lead to difficulties with chosen strategies, sending mixed messages and, in some cases, militating against efficiencies. Often it is given a geographical focus that may be inappropriate or irrelevant depending on the business you are in.

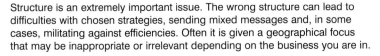

'Structure follows strategy' was a maxim coined by Alfred Chandler in 1962 *(Strategy and Structure)* by which he meant, that if the strategy is right, the structure would 'pop out' (form follows function).

It is now generally recognised that, in most cases, this is untrue and structure needs to be pro-actively managed to optimise strategy delivery. Whilst a better structure will not necessarily lead to a better organisation, a bad structure will be harmful. It is always right therefore to improve the structure.

Types of structure include: geographical, markets, products, functional and distribution. You should have the right structure to support the strategy. Often this resolves into a matrix for complex organisations.

9 DO IT!

Key points – This is about making it happen.

Key questions – Who will take responsibility for it? What is the critical path? What resources are required, initially and thereafter?

Actions – Allocate responsibilities to staff. May require new product/solution development. Communicate to stakeholders. Cascade responsibility down as appropriate.

Tools – RACI analysis, critical path (PERT) analysis, programme management, variance analysis, change management, communication media.

9 Do it!

STRATEGIC TOOLS

ADJUNCTS TO ANALYSIS

Tools are just that – they are a means of carrying out analysis in a structured manner. They are not the answers in themselves and should be used carefully, precisely and where appropriate. Using them for their own sake is a waste of time. Some of the more common tools include:

- SWOT analysis
- PEST analysis
- Scenario analysis
- Core competency analysis
- Critical Success Factor analysis

There are others, and most strategy books will either refer to these or contain variations on these and others. Many organisations have developed their own portfolio of tools and techniques, often portraying the results in a series of tables or 2 x 2 matrices...

GRIDS

Generally, 2 x 2 or 3 x 3 grids are frequently used in strategic analysis (Boston matrix, Ansoff matrix, Scenarios). Psychologically the brain can cope easily with the two dimensions that are represented in such a manner and it is a good medium for getting concepts across.

It must be remembered, however, that these grids are merely **simplified pictures of outputs**. They are not a means in themselves, but a method of presenting the findings or options that emerge from complex analysis.

They must not be taken at face value, instead the supporting data must be considered. Too often the grids are filled out superficially, rather than as a result of analysis, and the assumptions underpinning them are insufficiently challenged and probed.

Deciding to sell a subsidiary just because it appears as a 'dog' in a Boston matrix (see page 93) may be a costly error if the analysis is sketchy, data poor or incomplete and the industry cycle not considered (eg many start-ups appear as 'dogs' or 'problem children').

SWOT

SWOT stands for **S**trengths, **W**eaknesses, **O**pportunities and **T**hreats and can be a helpful way of classifying key issues. It **is only a list** and action must be taken to achieve lasting beneficial results:

Strengths – What you are good at, not in your opinion but in the objectively and empirically proven view of external third parties (eg many banks mistakenly assumed their customers were loyal because they mistook inertia for loyalty and were then surprised when many deserted to other institutions). A strength is where you have a recognised advantage that you can exploit.

Weaknesses – Those aspects which your customers tell you your competitors do better than you (eg why they bought X's product as a replacement for yours). Also, aspects that your customers/staff tell you need development.

Opportunities – Exploitable areas where you can use your strengths or where you can improve one of your weaknesses in order to make money.

Threats – Those things that might happen to your disadvantage in the market place (eg goods substitution, new low-cost competitor, new trend that changes consumer behaviour, legal changes, technological obsolescence, etc).

STRATEGIC TOOLS

PEST

PEST stands for **P**olitical/legal, **E**conomic, **S**ociocultural and **T**echnological. (**PESTLE** is a variant with **L**egal and **E**nvironmental issues separated out.) It is essentially an analysis of the external environment within which you must operate and which might influence your offerings. It enables a categorisation of the key factors that you believe will have an influence in the future. (Note that analysis of past impacts is only useful as a means of predicting or understanding future impacts.) The key factors can then be prioritised and the magnitude taken into account. PEST analysis is a vital input into such things as Scenario analysis:

Political	**Economic**	**Sociocultural**	**Technological**
Anti-trust laws	Economic cycles	Demography	R&D spend
Green laws	GNP	Income trends	Rate of change
Tax	Inflation	Education	Communications
Employment law	Interest rates	Lifestyles	Speed of transfer
Government	Unemployment	Fashions	
Behaviour	Energy prices	Mobility	

PORTER – FIVE FORCES

Michael Porter (Harvard professor) has, arguably, been one of the most influential strategic thinkers and writers this century. With the publication of his book *Competitive Strategy* in 1980 he became the definitive strategist of the twentieth century, with the book being required reading on all MBA courses and for business students generally.

The book focuses on a series of techniques for analysing industries and competitors and is still regarded as a seminal work. In it he argues that there are **five forces** shaping strategy within industries:

1. Rivalry amongst firms
2. Threat of substitute products
3. Threat of new entrants
4. Bargaining power of suppliers
5. Bargaining power of buyers

The relative strengths of these forces determine the profit of an industry which is, of course, different in each industry. The thrust of his book is that an organisation needs to understand these forces and then adopt a position from which to defend itself against them and influence the factors in its favour.

COMPETITIVE INTENSITY (AFTER PORTER)

Example analysis (output):

Level of competition / Five forces	LOW	MEDIUM	HIGH
Rivalry amongst firms			◯
Threat of new entrants		◯	
Bargaining power of buyers	◯		
Bargaining power of suppliers			◯
Threat of substitute products	◯		
Overall		◯	

Illustrative data only

PORTER – STRATEGIC OPTIONS

Porter then goes on to state that there are only three types of strategic options which organisations can use:

Differentiation – make your offering such that it is perceived as being unique and different from the rest.

Cost leadership – basically sell on price but with such tight cost controls that you are profitable.

Focus – deal only in a specific market or geographical location.

According to Porter, failure to follow one of these three options leaves you floundering 'somewhere in the middle'.

ANSOFF'S FIVE TURBULENCE LEVELS

Igor Ansoff, a long respected strategic thinker, has carried out much research into organisations' strategies. He has concluded that a major factor is that of **turbulence** – ie the changes through which a market is going – which can invalidate strategies. Understanding turbulence is of critical importance and may demand new approaches.

He categorises markets by the change through five states from *'repetitive'* (with little or no change) through to *'surpriseful'* where any planning may be totally invalidated (see over).

Each state will require a different type of strategic approach to meet the market trends and deliver value. This may differ for different units/offerings of the organisation, as will the rate of change. It is therefore important that the relative state of turbulence is understood **for each offering**.

Organisational analysis where offerings are positioned in different markets is pointless.

ANSOFF'S FIVE TURBULENCE LEVELS

STATE		**APPROACH**
1	Repetitive	Stable – procedural
2	Expanding	Reactive – control, budgets
3	Changing	Anticipatory – extrapolating long-term planning based on past
4	Discontinuous	Entrepreneurial – not based on past, strategic planning
5	Surpriseful	Creative – issue management, surprise management (contingency), hunch, gut feel, visionary leadership

Increasing turbulence

Each state requires a different approach to strategy and the state of your firm and its offerings must be known to enable you to develop the correct strategy.

STRATEGIC TOOLS

SCENARIO ANALYSIS

This is a technique that can help you address and understand the uncertainty that is implicit in future analysis.

- **Scenarios** are only as good as the information that supports them which, therefore, needs to be high quality

- They are not a forecast

- They seek to identify long-term forces and events and assess the likely impacts

- They help to focus limited internal resources to meet potentially unlimited challenges, but

- You need to choose carefully the factors that create the scenario/s.

'Predictions are very difficult to make, especially as regards the future.'
Chinese saying.

SCENARIO ANALYSIS

A scenario is defined as, 'an outline of future development which shows the operation of causes'.

- It describes a possible future – but is not a prediction
- It challenges current business model and thinking
- It must be engaging, interesting challenging and credible
- It must be logically consistent
- It is broader in scope and considers longer time horizons than a mere forecast

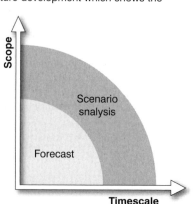

SCENARIO ANALYSIS

CRITICALITY VS UNCERTAINTY

In scenario analysis you develop a list of probable impacts on the business and then categorise them by the *degree of impact* versus the *likelihood* that they will impact.

This allows you to parcel the impacts up into:

- **Insignificant** – do not worry about these

- **Inevitable** – they will happen anyway so just be prepared to negate or exploit

- **Critically uncertain** – you need to develop action plans to address these within your defined scenarios

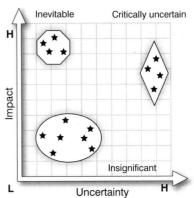

SCENARIO ANALYSIS

FACTORS AND DETERMINANTS

The four key factors that form a framework for scenario planning are:

1. **Social dynamics** – including quantitative demographics, lifestyle changes and political nuances
2. **Economic issues** – macroeconomic trends and forces shaping the economy
3. **Technological issues** – changes in technology/software, growing awareness of that change, greater enablers (internet etc), penetration by PCs of market
4. **Regulatory issues** – where and how and when will government (national/EU) intervene, taxation, controls

You must decide which are the key issues in each of the four factors and then, by contrasting one against another, a range of different scenarios can be developed. Eg Social dynamics V Economic, or Economic V Technology.

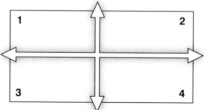

BOSTON MATRIX

One of the most famous tools was developed by the Boston Consulting Group (BCG). It looks at market growth and market share.

The **four** quadrants are:
A   **Low** growth **Low** market share
B   **Low** growth **High** market share
C   **High** growth **Low** market share
D   **High** growth **High** market share

Emotive icons are allocated to the quadrants:
A   Is usually a **dog**
B   Is a cash **cow**
C   Is a **question mark (problem child)**
D   Is allocated a **star**

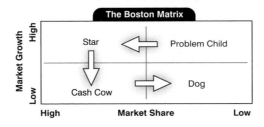

BOSTON MATRIX

The matrix is, of course, simplistic and inherently flawed. It is usually impossible to compare strategic business units from different organisations and assess the market share of each. For example, the retail unit of one bank will be competing against many different firms (such as building societies, utilities, life companies, retailers etc) each of which will have different product ranges and operate in different regional, national and, possibly, global markets.

When applied to products, however, this approach can be useful – even with its flaws. Products are more genuinely comparative across organisations, as are their markets.

CORE COMPETENCY ANALYSIS

This is about understanding the things that your organisation does well, and not so well, in the context of your offerings. You may well have a different profile for each offering and, if you wish to continue with them, you will need to ensure that your competencies support each.

The diagrams on the next page show two offerings with different competency profiles, indicating where action needs to be taken.

CORE COMPETENCY ANALYSIS

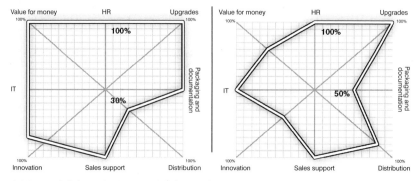

(100% = delight, 50 – 75% = satisfy, <50% = dissatisfy).

CORE COMPETENCIES RELATED TO OFFERINGS

Key issues with core competencies are: how flexible they are (How easy is it for you to respond to market change?) and how difficult it is for competitors to replicate them (Do you have strategic advantage?).

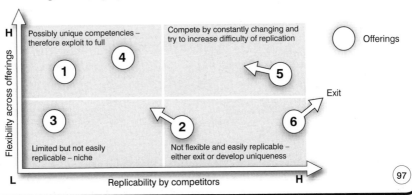

TREND ANALYSIS

Understanding the major trends in your sector and the forces causing them (see examples below) enables you to develop plans for countering/exploiting them.

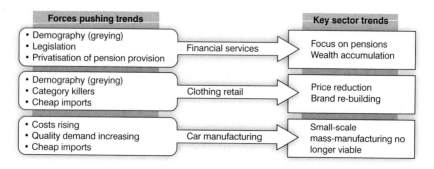

Forces pushing trends		Key sector trends
• Demography (greying) • Legislation • Privatisation of pension provision	Financial services	Focus on pensions Wealth accumulation
• Demography (greying) • Category killers • Cheap imports	Clothing retail	Price reduction Brand re-building
• Costs rising • Quality demand increasing • Cheap imports	Car manufacturing	Small-scale mass-manufacturing no longer viable

BUSINESS IMPACT ASSESSMENT

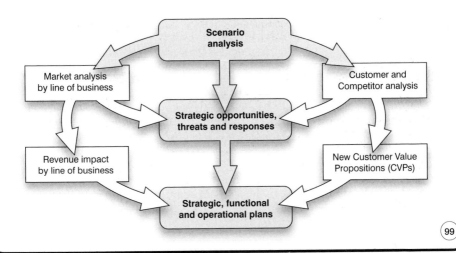

NOTES

TIPS

RISK

Risk is an ever present issue whenever strategy is developed. You must understand your potential risks. Too often risk is considered as adequately compensated for by reward – but too often it slips down the risk/reward line.

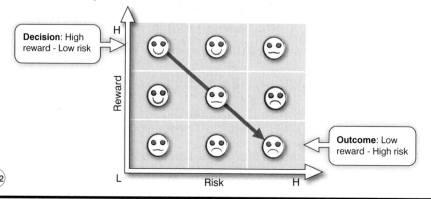

Decision: High reward - Low risk

Outcome: Low reward - High risk

Reward

Risk

H

L

H

ACCEPTABLE RISKS VS ACCEPTED RISKS

It is important to understand which risks you are taking – and those risks that you should be taking.

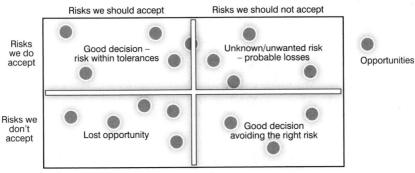

Adapted from Croft et al, Management and Organisation in Financial Services, IFS.

CRITICAL SUCCESS FACTORS (CSFs)

It is important to compare your strategy with the CSFs. Does it hit all or most of them? If not, you are likely to fail.

Strategic action	Business objectives					CSFs				Overall
	A	B	C	D	E					
1	●	●		◐		◐	◐	○	●	◐
2	○	○		●			◐	◐		○
3		○	●		◐	●		◐	◐	●
4	◐	●		◐	●	●	●		◐	◐
5	○		◐			○	○	●		○
6										
7										
8										

 Supports partially   Fully aligned   No impact

(104)

Illustrative data only

PITFALLS

Bureaucratisation – Too many organisations leave strategy to bureaucratic planning departments. Reams of paper produced but no action!

Complexity – Often too much focus on trying to plan and manage the whole organisation rather than the organisation as a whole.

Paralysis of analysis – Follows too much refinement and iteration. Usually reflects an inability to make decisions or lack of clarity over vision, goals and targets.

Too much involvement at wrong levels – Allocated to junior staff or departments rather than having senior executive involvement in formulation.

Planning by numbers – OK as far as it goes, but strategy requires more vision and inspiration, supported by 'perspiration' to prove the concept.

TIPS

PITFALLS

Outsourcing your strategic development – Many organisations hand over strategy lock, stock and barrel to 'strategy' firms. As a result they never develop the proper understanding of development and implementation, and are dependent time and time again on the outsiders 'doing their strategy' for them.

Forecasting too far into the future – The further out you go, the less accurate forecasts are. Better to carry out scenario analysis rather than long-term forecasts.

Confusing *fundamental* objectives and *means* objectives – Don't confuse the things that you really want to achieve (fundamental) and those things you need to achieve on the way.

Lack of clarity – Know the difference between corporate strategy and competitive strategies.

TO SUCCEED YOU MUST...

- Be totally clear as to the vision
- Understand your markets and offering, as well as the competition and trends
- Be clear about your offering and draw up your competitive strategy for chosen segments. Do not compete where you can't make money!

- Ensure that the support functions have clear goals that are aligned to strategic goals, and resources and management necessary to achieve them
- Put in place clear targets to measure progress towards goals
- Be flexible to changes in markets
- Add value to all groups of stakeholders – relative to their importance

Achievement of strategic goals and targets

FURTHER READING

BOOKS

There are literally hundreds of books on strategy. Some of the more helpful are listed below:

Strategic Safari
Henry Mintzberg
Published by FT – Prentice Hall (1998)

Strategic Planning
Igor Ansoff
Published by John Wiley & Sons (1976)

Competitive Advantage
Michael E. Porter
Published by The Free Press (2004)

Mastering Strategy Series
Financial Times editors et al
Published by FT – Prentice Hall

It may also be helpful to contact the Strategic Planning Society www.sps.org.uk who also publish a quarterly magazine through Elsevier, *'LRP – long range planning'*.

About the Author

Neil Russell-Jones BSc (Hons), MBA, ACIB is an author and management consultant and a member of the Strategic Planning Society. He is also a part-time lecturer in Strategy/Business Studies at Thames Valley University.

He works internationally with many organisations in many countries assisting them in developing or testing strategy, in improving their performance, change/programme management and in market analysis/research.

He has written many books and papers on business topics. His other titles include for Management Pocketbooks: *Business Planning, Decision-making, Strategy,* and *Marketing*; and for the Institute of Financial Services: *Customer Relationship Management, Risk Evaluation, Customers and Their Needs* and *Marketing, Sales and Customer Service*.

He has been a lecturer on the CASS EMBA course, and a special advisor for the Prince's Youth Business Trust (patron HRH the Prince of Wales) in the areas of strategy and marketing. Neil is a regular speaker in many countries and has often appeared on radio and TV in the UK and elsewhere.

You can contact him at neil.jones@eponaconsulting.com

ORDER FORM

Your details

Name _____

Position _____

Company _____

Address _____

_____

_____

Telephone _____

Fax _____

E-mail _____

VAT No. (EC companies) _____

Your Order Ref _____

Please send me:

No. copies

The _Strategy_____ Pocketbook ☐

The _____ Pocketbook ☐

The _____ Pocketbook ☐

The _____ Pocketbook ☐

Order by Post

MANAGEMENT POCKETBOOKS LTD

LAUREL HOUSE, STATION APPROACH,
ALRESFORD, HAMPSHIRE SO24 9JH UK

Order by Phone, Fax or Internet

Telephone: +44 (0)1962 735573
Facsimile: +44 (0)1962 733637
E-mail: sales@pocketbook.co.uk
Web: www.pocketbook.co.uk

Customers in USA should contact:

Management Pocketbooks

2427 Bond Street, University Park, IL 60466
Telephone: 866 620 6944 Facsimile: 708 534 7803
E-mail: mp.orders@ware-pak.com
Web: www.managementpocketbooks.com